Rough-coated sheepdogs found employment all over Europe.

OLD FARM DOGS

David Hancock

Shire Publications

Contents

ACKNOWLEDGEMENTS
Illustrations are acknowledged as follows: Abbot Hall Art Gallery, Kendal, pages 16 (top), 18 (bottom); Bibliothèque Nationale, Paris, page 7 (top); Centre for Oxfordshire Studies, page 13 (top right and centre); Charwynne Dog Features, pages 4 (both), 5 (top), 6 (both), 7 (centre and bottom), 8 (both), 9 (both), 10 (bottom three), 11 (both), 13 (top left), 14 (bottom), 15 (top), 16 (bottom), 17 (top two), 18 (top), 20, 21 (all), 22 (top two), 23, 25 (top), 26 (all), 27 (all), 28, 29, 30, 31, cover; Czartoryska, page 22 (bottom); Dorset County Museum, page 3; Thomas Fall, page 24; Miss E. Gallatly, page 1; Lana Lou Lane, page 19 (bottom); Museum of East Anglian Life, page 32; Museum of Welsh Life, pages 5 (bottom), 15 (bottom); Norfolk Museums Service, Norfolk Rural Life Museum, Gressenhall, pages 17 (bottom), 19 (top); Mevr. A. H. de Raad, page 25 (bottom); Staffordshire County Museum, page 10 (top); Suffolk Record Office, page 12. The illustration on page 14 (top) is from W. H. Pyne, *The Costumes of Great Britain* (1808).

Cover: *A shepherd with an English sheepdog of a type common in the south of England, c.1820. (Unknown artist of naïve school.)*

British Library Cataloguing in Publication Data: Hancock, David. Old farm dogs. – (Shire album; no. 345) 1. Working dogs – Great Britain – History I. Title 636.7'3'0941. ISBN 0 7478 0429 X.

Published in 1999 by Shire Publications Ltd, Cromwell House, Church Street, Princes Risborough, Bucking-hamshire HP27 9AA, UK. (Website: www.shirebooks.co.uk)
Copyright © 1999 by David Hancock. First published 1999. Shire Album 345. ISBN 0 7478 0429 X.
David Hancock is hereby identified as the author of this work in accordance with Section 77 of the Copyright, Designs and Patents Act 1988.

Printed in Great Britain by CIT Printing Services Ltd, Press Buildings, Merlins Bridge, Haverfordwest, Pembrokeshire SA61 1XF.

Nat Seal, a Dorset drover who died in 1898, with his working sheepdog. On the subject of the drover's dog, Youatt, in his 'The Dog' of 1854, wrote: 'He bears considerable resemblance to the Sheepdog, and has usually the same prevailing black or brown colour. He possesses all the docility of the Sheepdog, with more courage, and sometimes ferocity.' Some of them, from injudicious crossing, 'are as much like Setters, Lurchers, and hounds as the original breed'.

Introduction

Britain's sporting dogs have had whole libraries of books devoted to them, reflecting perhaps the education and wealth of those who use them. Books on spaniels, setters, pointers, beagles and foxhounds, describing their training, husbandry and breeding, fill the shelves of many a country house. But books on working dogs, that is dogs which serve the farmer, are relatively rare. The value of such dogs, however, both to the farmer and to the nation is indisputable. Their fame has spread throughout the world, with no other nation producing a breed of dog with the skill, intelligence and working wisdom of Britain's premier farm dog, the Border Collie. Britain's other pastoral breeds have earned fame too, from the acting ability of Rough Collie 'Lassie' on cinema screens to the patronage of the once humble Corgi by the royal family.

Obedience and agility championship shows are open to any breed; they are dominated, however, by the Border Collie developed by farmers, not by breeds developed by the nobility. We owe a great debt to farmers' dogs, for their centuries of service, whether protecting lambs, getting stock to markets or finding straying stock on freezing, windswept hillsides. Not for them the indulgence of sport to amuse their masters but the serious business of working daily in any conditions to fulfil a role neither man nor machine can match. Despite this unique service to man, most breeds of farm dog are now lost to us: we seem to prefer exotic breeds with less worthy origins – and shame on us for that.

A fresco found at Sefar in the Sahara and dating from around 2000 BC. The use of dogs as herders is clearly depicted (top and bottom).

The farmer's needs

Most breeds of pastoral dog evolved over the centuries out of the needs of farmers worldwide, whether static or nomadic, to protect, control, drive, herd, pen, heel or even 'pin' cattle, sheep, pigs, goats, reindeer or other animals being 'farmed'.

Not surprisingly, the breeds that *protected* flocks of sheep from wild predators, human rustlers or other dogs were large and fierce. Those that *controlled* the flock or herd were smaller, more biddable and, although less fierce, were still very determined, such as the German Shepherd Dog, which was used as a 'living fence'. The *driving* breeds combined stamina and robustness with an instinctive desire to keep the flock or herd together as a group. The *herding* or *penning* breeds were required to be highly responsive to the human voice or whistle and yet still be very strong-willed. British breeds have always excelled in this role. The *heeling* breeds were used to turn or drive cattle and had to be small, quick and alert, as the Corgi breeds demonstrate today. The *pinning* or *gripping* breeds, once hunting breeds and used extensively by butchers, were needed to seize and hold one individual animal, for example a powerful sow, to facilitate handling or even slaughter. Broad-mouthed dogs such as the Bullmastiff, were used for this type of work.

A Cotswold shepherd with a Bearded Collie c.1890. The sheep-herding breeds were bred for performance, not for type.

4

The sheepdogs of the Caucasus: flock guardians at work – powerful dogs with thick protective coats.

The pastoral breeds may have dominated the farm dog scene all over the world, but farmers had other needs too. Dangerous and persistent predators such as the fox and the coyote had to be hunted down and controlled if farming was to be viable. In Britain, for example, farmers sometimes kept or supported 'bobbery' packs of assorted hounds to hunt foxes, just as American farmers use huge lurchers (which they call staghounds) to hunt coyote. Farm buildings and ricks attracted vermin, which also had to be controlled. Ratting terriers were therefore valued, although collies, and especially heelers, carried out this task too. Farmers prized their dogs for their functional ability and only bred good worker to good worker, thus concentrating instinctive skills. The purely cosmetic appeal of a dog, so valued nowadays, was superfluous to the hard-working farmer.

It was during the eighth and seventh millennia BC that man first began to domesticate sheep and goats within the region of western Asia. Unlike nomadic animals such as gazelles, antelope and bison, humans, sheep, goats and dogs were all part of a social system based on a single dominant leader and tended to settle on what became known as a home range. They therefore become interdependent, with the herdsman as leader and the dog his agent. Dogs also protected humans and their livestock against wild predators such as lynxes, lions, wolves, tigers, jackals,

Local farmers foxhunting near Llyn Ogwen, Gwynedd, in the 1930s. The multi-purpose farm collie was part of the team.

5

Controlling vermin was a constant need in farmhouses, farm buildings and ricks. This terrier, nondescript and workmanlike, illustrates the farmer's preference for function over beauty.

leopards, cheetahs, foxes, civets and, in some places, huge eagles. Flock-guarding dogs therefore had to be brave, vigilant, determined, alert, resolute and, above all, protective.

Their role, the climate and the terrain demanded excellent feet, tough frames, weatherproof coats, great stamina, good hearing and eyesight and remarkable robustness. These dogs operated in harsh conditions, ranging from the hottest to the coldest, the stoniest, thorniest, windiest, most mountainous and most arid areas of Europe and western Asia. Farmers and shepherds had to have entirely functional dogs: physical exaggeration does not occur in any of the flock-guarding breeds, unlike in ornamental dogs. Hunting ability was not desired, although the physical

Bob-tailed sheepdogs depicted at the end of the nineteenth century. There is no attempt to glamorise them. They do look like real working dogs.

Left: *A mountain dog or flock-guarding dog (as portrayed in the Bibliothèque Nationale, Paris). The impressive stature of the dog is typical of the flock-guarding breeds.*

Below: *The Lappland herding dog displays the thick coat required by a pastoral dog in Arctic conditions.*

power and bravery of such dogs did lead to their use in bear hunts in Russia and boar hunts in central Europe, where they were used at the kill, not as scenthounds.

The demands of climate have led to both the flock guardians and the shepherd dogs featuring appropriate coats for their region. The Hungarian Komondor and the Italian Bergamasco display the thick, felted coats required to survive in their working environment. The French Beauceron and the New Zealand Huntaway exhibit the smooth, sleek coats best suited to their climate.

If we then look at the short legs

This French Beauceron exhibits the smoother coat that is favourable to their use and location.

Left: *The goat-haired sheepdogs illustrate how coat length and texture, size and working style developed out of the farmer's needs. This photograph of a cowherd in northern England was taken by the Reverend James Pattison c.1901.*

Below: *The courage of a 30 pound (13.6 kg) collie in facing a bullock weighing three-quarters of a tonne is often underrated.*

of the heeling breeds and the longer legs of Belgian, Dutch and German shepherd dogs, we can see how not only climate but also terrain and function determined type. In some areas the goat-haired breeds like the Bearded Collie were favoured, because of the local conditions and their instinctive skills. The breeds were shaped by the farmers' needs.

Wherever they worked or farmed, farmers needed dogs with the innate characteristics, the appropriate physique and the suitable length and texture of coat to protect, drive or herd their stock, hunt down vermin and guard their farmsteads. Their demanding requirements have given us some of the most popular breeds of companion dog today, although sadly these are bred more with cosmetic than functional considerations in today's society. The advent of dog shows towards the end of the nineteenth century meant that, for the first time in man's long association with dog, a dog from a working breed could be valued more for its looks than for what it could do.

The working sheepdog has changed little during the twentieth century, as this 1910 portrayal indicates.

Roles and types

There were so many breeds of farm dog in the Kennel Club group called the Working Group that it became necessary to form a specific group, the Pastoral Group, just for these. Nearly forty thousand dogs of breeds from this group are newly registered each year with the Kennel Club, and four of the twenty most popular breeds are in the Pastoral Group. Around seven thousand working sheep-dog puppies are also registered annually with the International Sheepdog Society, with twice that number again being unregistered. But the popularity of some breeds has been accompanied by the loss of others. Just as in the past the development of the railways removed the need for drovers, so too will the economic pressures on hill farmers and the evolution of an increasingly urban society reduce the demand for dogs to work livestock.

It is difficult to visualise nowadays six thousand sheep being moved on foot in more or less one huge flock from east of the Pennines to the markets of Norwich and Smithfield. It is not easy to think of thousands of cattle, sheep and even geese being shepherded by a small number of dogs from remote rural pastures along estab-lished drove-roads to city markets – and the dogs then being left to find their own way home. Today's hill walker, benefiting from specially developed clothing, detailed

A team of dogs has long been invaluable for working a large flock of sheep, as this 1912 photograph illustrates.

The Old English Sheepdog has the steady ambling gait of the long-distance walker.

maps, an accurate compass and high-energy foods, still faces challenges from the harsh terrain and unforgiving weather of mountainous areas in which sheepdogs and cattle dogs have operated effectively for centuries. These are very remarkable dogs.

In medieval times livestock were protected by huge dogs known as shepherds' mastiffs, the word *mastiff* being used here to describe a large mongrel, not in the modern sense of a pedigree breed. As large wild predators disappeared from Britain, the need for such dogs disappeared too, but the Old English Sheepdog type may well have descended from such dogs.

As the forested areas were reduced, the dogs of the forest shepherd had to find a new role; it is likely that the working sheepdog or collie of today comes from such dogs. In some areas it was customary to use multi-purpose dogs on farms, such as in Ireland, where the versatile Kerry Blue and soft-coated Wheaten Terrier were stock dogs, farm terriers and guard dogs. Drovers needed to feed themselves on their long journeys and used a sheepdog cross greyhound, known as a lurcher, to fill their pots with meat. The Smooth Collie is considered by some experts to have developed from such a cross.

Above left: *The soft-coated Wheaten Terrier of Ireland typifies the versatile all-purpose farm dog: drover, ratter and guard.*

Above right: *Robert Chapman's smooth-coated collie 'Young Trim' portrayed in 1891. It was more like a Border Collie.*

Right: *A long-haired ratting terrier of the nineteenth century, somewhat resembling the contemporary soft-coated Wheaten Terrier. It could be used with sheep and may have had sheepdog blood.*

The 'header–stalker' dogs, like this working Scottish collie of c.1920, used instincts passed down from their wild ancestors.

Big, flock-guarding dogs are still used in countries where sheep are pastured in remote mountain areas. Charles Darwin, on a South American tour, noted how such dogs were trained from puppyhood for their future role. The flockmaster taught the pups how to be suckled by a ewe, sleep in a nest of wool and progress to expect meat at the end of the day at a set location, where the sheep would accompany them. Puppies of the sheep-guarding breeds slept with the lambs and sometimes adult bitches allowed lambs to suckle from them. Dog and sheep bonded from such activities.

In this role, a certain type of dog is needed. The dog's instinct to defend its territory is harnessed to guard a pasture. The dog then, without human direction, places itself between an approaching predator and the stock in its remote pasture. This is in stark contrast with the herding breeds – hyperactive dogs that stalk, chase, bully, bark at and even bite sheep to impose their will on them. These are the 'header–stalkers', using classic canine predatory behaviour inherited from wild ancestors. They usually feature the prick ears and long muzzles of those wild forebears. These dogs have to be controlled by human voice or whistle.

It is likely that dogs such as the Bobtail or Old English Sheepdog in southern England and the Beardie or Bearded Collie in northern England and Scotland were the flock guardians and then the drovers' dogs. When a sizeable flock was being patrolled by dogs at night, each dog could be located by the shepherd through its distinctive bark. The Bearded Collie gives tongue when working, unlike its relative, the Border Collie, or working sheepdog, as the

An early photograph of a Cotswold shepherd and a Bearded Sheepdog, a breed which 'gives tongue' or barks, when working.

Suffolk shepherds with their collies: collies with these characteristics have hardly changed in centuries.

unregistered ones tend to be called. The Old English Sheepdog has the steady, ambling, energy-saving gait of the long-distance walker; the Bearded Collie, which was expected to herd too, has a quicker, effortless, gliding walk. An old grazier on Salisbury Plain recalled in the 1950s how the instinctive skills of his Bobtails varied: some preferred to lead sheep, others to drive them as a flock and others again to guard a flank. This behaviour occurred in young untrained dogs. The Bobtail excelled as a stockyard guard. The Old English Sheepdog and the Bearded Collie, both heavier-coated breeds, were shorn with the sheep and salved with a mixture of tar and oil as an insect-repellent and weather-proofer. Both were very much outdoor breeds!

No old print, painting or photograph depicts these heavier-coated breeds with the excessive length of coat displayed by many of their successors in today's show rings. Too heavy or too long a coat is a needless imposition on a working dog. Early in the twentieth century, Henry Tilley, who contributed so much to the development of the Old English Sheepdog, wrote: 'During recent years there has been an increasing tendency to over-development of the coat and especially for show purposes, but it is an adverse handicap for "working" dogs, which are exposed to all weathers, mud, and dusty roads.'

In 1949, the working sheepdog expert James Garrow wrote to Mrs G. O. Willison, who launched the show career of the Bearded Collie:

> The Beardie was essentially a worker, famed for fleetness and brains, kept by butchers, farmers, etc... The coat should not be overlong and of a raw harsh texture... Have you drawn up the standard for the KC [the Kennel club] yet? You want to emphasise the rule on coat.

Most of the Beardies in the show ring these days display such a length of silky coat as to obscure the natural lines of the dog's body, contrary to the wording of the breed standard, although the standard for the Old English Sheepdog places no

Above: *This Oxfordshire shepherd's dog was very much of the type that graduated to the show ring.*

Left: *The working Bearded Collie never displayed the heavy over-long coat of today's show-ring specimens.*

This Oxfordshire farm dog represents the type that became known as the 'Blue Shag' in Hampshire.

restriction on the length of coat.

It has been claimed that Peeblesshire is the home of the true Beardie and Dorset that of the Bobtail. But bob-tailed sheepdogs were known in Scotland too, and Beardies have long been favoured south of the border in north-west England. Breeds utilised by drovers could be found wherever there was a thriving sheep trade. The Smithfield Sheepdog, a bigger Beardie, was associated not just with the market of that name but with the market towns of eastern England too. In Hampshire, a bearded sheepdog called a Blue Shag was favoured. In Wales, the Old Welsh Grey or Bearded Hillman was the choice.

13

The Highland shepherd relied on his collie not only for guiding his flock into the best pastures but also at sheep-counting time.

Beardies work in a different style from that of their shorter-haired fellow working sheepdogs. They are not silent or 'strong-eyed' but excel at collecting and then retaining sheep in big groups. This capability made them most useful to drovers and butchers at markets. In the early days of trying to breed pure Beardies it was not unusual to find a couple of pups in a litter looking more like Border Collies. The early registrations of sheepdogs with the International Sheepdog Society, which looks after the interests of the working dogs, listed rough, smooth and bearded types. But farmers often inter-bred dogs with different coats and ear carriage in the pursuit of the best workers for their pastures.

Cumbrian sheep farmer Malcolm Ewart of Barketh Farm near Bassenthwaite Lake works Beardies on grazing stints on Skiddaw around 3000 feet (900 metres) above sea level. He has a waiting list for his pups, so highly are his dogs rated as workers. But his dogs do not feature the length of coat seen on show-ring specimens of the breed. Show breeders may not want their dogs to work on Skiddaw, but if the dogs are true Bearded Collies they should be physically able to do so. Every pedigree Bearded Collie in the world registered as such can be traced back to one of just twelve dogs, a tiny genetic base. This admirable breed will need wise breeders if it is to retain its robustness, virility and characteristics.

Just as the Beardie combined the skills of driving and herding, the shorter-coated working sheepdog, usually described as a collie, using the 'header–stalker' technique rather than that of the flock guardian, not only matched them but suited the changing ways of farming. As the development of the railways did away with the need for drovers and the acreage of common grazing land de-creased, there was a need for dogs able to move stock from one fenced pasture to another, pen them for shearing and health checks and get them on to vehicles for market. It is likely that these shorter-coated farm collies were not widely used in Wales and southern England until the livestock industry adapted to new transport opportunities.

In the far north of the British Isles were the Kelpies (leggy dogs used to get grazing stock out to small islands at low tide) of the Orkneys, the bigger Scottish collies (with their rough, smooth and bearded variants) of the Highlands, and what we now call Border Collies in the Lowlands and northernmost English counties. Shetland had its own type, which was smaller

A strongly built, thick-coated working sheepdog, with its farmer owners, pictured in the last quarter of the nine-teenth century.

The old black-and-tan sheepdog was favoured in central Wales and the north of Scotland.

and more of a house dog. Cumberland, too, had its own sheepdog, looking more like a German Shepherd Dog (in size if not in coat colour) than its own collie relatives. The original Border Collie type may have been the forest sheepdogs (referred to as 'ramhunts' in some accounts) used to keep stock in clearings, constantly circling them to keep the flock together and deter predators. In time, selective breeding developed these instinctive skills, leading to such dogs becoming the national herding breed.

In Wales, there were distinct types like the Welsh Hillman, a handsome red-coated dog, the Black-and-Tan Sheepdog and the Welsh Collie, often predominantly white. A pure strain of all-black, or black-and-tan, sometimes chocolate or bronze coloured, collie was once favoured in Sutherland and Ross, with some experts linking them with Scandinavian herding dogs.

A passage from W. H. Pyne's *The Costumes of Great Britain* of 1808 provides some insight into the life of a Highland shepherd:

> The dog, by being constantly the companion of the Highland shepherd, acquires sagacity, far superior to what is common to the brute creation; appearing to comprehend all his master's commands... The shepherd, who is acquainted with the best spots for pasture, and who watches for prognostics of the weather, manages the flock accordingly, by the aid of the dog, who drives the sheep sometimes to the summit of a mountain, and at other times, to a particular spot upon its side, or into a deep glen, acting by the signals of his master; who stands on a conspicuous height, shouting his directions, and waving his crook, which the intelligent animal comprehends at a surprising distance.

The ability of herding dogs to single out individual sheep is well attested. Pyne went on to describe this ability:

> The shepherd at the time of collecting the flock in the evening for the purpose of counting it, fixes his crook in the ground, and stands a few paces therefrom: the dog drives the sheep between the crook and his master, who numbers them as they pass; but if a straggler goes on the outside, and mixes with those who have passed muster, the dog immediately pursues, singles him out, and brings him back.

A further illustration comes in an anecdote in the Reverend Charles Williams's

Ellis Hughes, a shepherd at Glasfryn, in North Wales, with two Welsh Grey Sheepdogs and a Fox Terrier, the latter a farm vermin controller.

A black merle champion sheepdog from Westmorland posed with the cups he had won, c.1900.

Dogs and Their Ways of 1863:

> Lord Truro told Lord Brougham of a drover's dog, whose sagacious conduct he observed when he happened on one occasion to meet a drove. The man had brought seventeen out of twenty oxen from a field, leaving the remaining three there mixed with another herd. He then said to the dog, 'Go, fetch them,' and he went and singled out those very three.

In Ireland, the tricolour Galway Sheepdog, a strapping black, tan and white dog, and the Glenwherry Collie of Antrim, a wall-eyed merle dog, were favoured (a merle dog has a coat containing dark patches against a light background of the same basic colour, usually black patches on grey). In Leinster, particularly in County Wicklow, a red merle, bob-tailed collie was utilised. Merino sheep were imported into the Kilkenny area, together with a Spanish shepherd who used blasts on a horn to call his sheep.

When flocks of sheep were sold it was common practice to sell the dogs that managed them as well. In this way, many sheepdogs went from Britain to the colonies. This has led to British herding dogs becoming not only the most valued in the world, but adapted and developed into native breeds in their new countries. The Border Collie or working sheepdog of sheepdog trial fame is the best-known 'strong-eyed' breed in the world, so-called because it exerts control over sheep by assertive eye contact and aggressive body positioning.

But just as working collies were highly valued in Britain and other countries, so too were heelers. These small driving dogs, known to countrymen as 'nip 'n' duck' dogs, stimulated cattle into movement by nipping their heels and then flattening themselves to avoid the retaliatory kick. Heelers were a common sight in the seventeenth and eighteenth centuries. Rather as each county or region often had its own distinctive brand of terrier (the Cheshire White, the hound-marked Devonshire and the black and tan of Shropshire), so too it had its heeler. The Welsh heeler is perpetuated in the Pembrokeshire and Cardiganshire Corgis, originally more like leggy Dachshunds and often with drop ears, unlike the prick-eared dogs of today. The Norfolk heeler was of wheaten colour, rather similar to today's Norwich Terrier but longer in the leg. The Lancashire Heeler, a black-and-tan smooth-coated dog, was saved from extinction and achieved Kennel Club recognition in 1981. There was a version of this heeler in Ormskirk, with white on its chest.

The British 'strong-eyed' sheepdog is famous in farming circles throughout the world. This is a 1911 photograph.

16

Right: *The Cardiganshire Welsh Corgi, one of the Welsh heelers used to move cattle from farms to main drove-ways.*

In his *A General History of Quadrupeds* written in 1790, Thomas Bewick recorded:

> The Cur Dog is a trusty and useful servant to the farmer and grazier; and... such great attention is paid in breeding it, that we cannot help considering it as a permanent kind... They are chiefly employed in driving cattle... They bite very keenly; and as they always make their attack at the heels, the cattle have no defence against them.

The 'cur dog' described here is a heeler; the word *cur* is nowadays less than a compliment but it is clear from these words that it was not a term for any old dog!

In Spurrell's dictionary of the Welsh language, published in 1859, the meaning of corgi was given as 'cur-dog', either from *cur-ci* or *cor-ci, ci* meaning 'dog' and *cor* 'dwarf'. The two extant breeds of Welsh corgi show interesting differences. The Pembrokeshire dog is more like the spitz breeds of northern Europe. Some attribute this to a connection with the Vikings, who started settlements in that county and may have brought their Vallhund herders with them. Another view links this Welsh breed with the introduction by Flemish weavers of small dogs like the Belgian breed, the Schipperke. This breed is also tail-less and prick-eared; the original name may have been *Scheperke*, or shepherd, and some experts believe the breed to be a diminutive form of the black variety of the Belgian shepherd dog, the Groenendael. The Cardiganshire corgi is less spitz-like, with a full tail, and resembles a miniature version of the Welsh Hillman. Both these breeds carried out the vital task of getting cattle to the main drove-roads and preventing local stock from joining the herd. This done, the leggier dogs could escort them to the markets of England.

Further east, on the Monmouthshire–Herefordshire border in the Black Mountains, just north of Ewyas Harold, there is a collection of isolated farms where the farmers have preserved their own variety of heeler–sheepdog, which they call their bob-tail. Looking like a tail-less or stumpy-tailed Border Collie, they are reminiscent of the type written about in the *Modern Farrier* (various authors) in 1832: 'fiercer than the shepherd's dog; their hair is smoother and shorter. They are mostly of a black and

Above: *The Lancashire Heeler: the only surviving English breed of heeler.*

Below: *A shepherd in Norfolk in 1923 with his Smithfield Sheepdog, a type now lost, but still cropping up in lurchers.*

17

A little bob-tailed sheepdog bitch from the Black Mountains near Hereford: a sharp, enormously determined type of herding dog.

white colour; their ears are half-pricked; and many of them with short tails; which seem as if they had been cut. These are called self-tailed dogs.' The bob-tailed dogs of the Black Mountains are renowned for their hardness: they will 'grip' a troublesome ram by the neck, a bothersome bull by the nose and hang on a cow's tail in their utter determination to impose their will.

Heelers, with their advantage of being close to the ground, doubled up as rat-killers on farms, although many farms favoured the local breed of hunt terrier to do this work. Farmers in hill areas banded together to hunt their other main vermin, the fox. In Wales and the Lake District, there is a long tradition of foxhunting carried out by farmers banding together, often bringing their own hounds with them, to reduce the loss of lambs, especially to the big hill foxes. But it is more the norm for a motley or 'bobbery' pack of farm terriers and collies to do this work. A few farmers have been known to keep lurchers specifically bred for fox-coursing in countryside where long views abound. These dogs run the fox down in open country rather than run it to ground.

Dogs, both tiny and huge, had a role to play in the farmer's life. The smallest, shortest-legged heelers and terriers were sometimes employed as 'turnspits', running a treadmill to turn the spit in the farm kitchen or waterwheels at wells. 'Turnspit Tykes' became a distinct type, Queen Victoria having three at Windsor. They were still in use in Wales as late as 1870. At the other end of the size scale, powerful dogs were used to pull farm handcarts, especially in dairies, but never to the degree that draught dogs were used in towns, particularly on the Continent and mainly by butchers and other market traders.

Quite unlike any of these dogs, and now no longer employed in Britain, are the pinning or gripping dogs. These dogs, often cross-bred Bulldogs and ferociously determined, were the specialists at pinning cattle or

Westmorland collies of c.1900. Farm collies conformed to a type but not to a breed standard with precise wording.

Warreners at Barnham, Suffolk, in the early twentieth century with their lurchers, a collie greyhound cross.

This big Bulldog, used in America to 'pin' wayward cattle, illustrates the type of 'holding dog' used by farmers and butchers in Britain two hundred years ago. Hugh Dalziel, in his 'British Dogs' of 1897, recounted how 'some cattle were being driven through a butcher's shop in London, when one broke away from the rest, and could not be driven through the door. The butcher called his Bulldog, described as of the old-fashioned type, about 45 lb, which had been quietly watching the proceedings from the side of the shop, and the dog rushed immediately and seized the beast by the nose, and dragged it forcibly through the shop into the yard at the back.'

pigs. In Wales, they were known as the *Gafaelgi* or holding dogs. In Germany, they were known as *Bullenbeissers*, literally 'bull-biters'. Invaluable to butchers and stockmen as well as farmers in more primitive times, they instinctively seized a wayward sow by the ear or a bull by the nose or cheek as a way of restraining them. Originally they were the hunting mastiffs that pulled down big game for the hunter before firearms could do better. The Perro de Presa Canario or gripping dog of the Canaries and the British breed of Bullmastiff are living examples of such dogs.

The gripping or holding dogs performed a function required at that time. The biggest threat to the pastoral dog is not the passage of time and changes in agriculture but human whim. The glamorous Rough Collie may grace film sets, and the likeable Bobtail may star in paint advertisements, but neither breed works any more. The world famous and unsurpassable Border Collie now features in the show ring, but only after considerable opposition from the International Sheepdog Society, which rightly feared a loss of functional ability and working physique. These dogs may have moved from the pastures to city streets but really they are only spiritually happy when working and are too hyperactive to make good house pets. The challenge for their fanciers is to breed them for their new role without losing their essential characteristics, for that is how all breeds survive.

Old farm dogs around the world

From Portugal in the west, across to the Lebanon and on to the Caucasus mountains in the east, from southern Greece through Hungary to northern Russia, there are powerful pastoral dogs to be found, developed over thousands of years to protect man's domesticated animals from the attacks of wild animals. Some are called shepherd dogs, others mountain dogs and a few dubbed mastiffs, despite the conformation of their skulls. Their coat colours vary from pure white to wolf-grey and from a rich red to black-and-tan. Some are no longer used as herd-protectors, and their numbers in north-west Europe dramatically decreased when the use of draught dogs lapsed. A number of common characteristics link these widely separated breeds: a thick weatherproof coat, a powerful build, an independence of mind, a certain majesty and a strong instinct to protect. As a group, they would be most accurately described as the flock guardians.

In south-west Europe these dogs became known in time as breeds such as the Estrela mountain dog and the Rafeiro do Alentejo of Portugal and the Extremadura mastiff of Spain. To the north-east of the Iberian peninsula, such dogs became known as the Pyrenean Mountain Dog and, separately, as the Pyrenean 'Mastiff'. In the Alps they divided, as different regions favoured different coat colours and textures, into the *sennenhund* or mountain pasture breeds that we know today as the Bernese, Appenzell, Entlebuch and Great Swiss mountain dogs, and the St Bernard. In Italy, local shepherds favoured the pale colours now found in the Maremma sheepdog and the very heavy coat of the Bergamasco. In the Balkans, similarly differing preferences led to the emergence of the all-white Greek sheepdog and the wolf-grey flock guardians of the former Yugoslavia.

Further east, other breed-types were stabilised into the Kuvasz and Komondor of Hungary, the Rumanian sheepdog, the Tatra mountain sheepdog of Poland, the

A shepherd with his mountain dogs in the type of country where large, fierce guarding and herding dogs are required by virtue of the rugged terrain and the presence of predatory animals.

Right: *The Bergamasco, the flock guardian of Italy, showing the coat needed for winters in the mountains.*

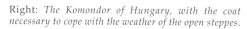
Above: *The Kurst sheepdog of Yugoslavia, the flock-guardian type found in the Balkans.*

Right: *The Komondor of Hungary, with the coat necessary to cope with the weather of the open steppes.*

Left: *The Kuvasz of Hungary, typifying the size and strength of the flock-guarding breeds.*

21

Slovakian Kuvasz, the Mendelan of north Russia and the Owtcharkas of south Russia and the Caucasus. In the Himalayan regions appeared the so-called Tibetan 'Mastiff', the Bhotia, the Bisben, the Bangara mastiff, the Koochi or Powinder dog of Afghanistan and the Powendah dog of north-west Pakistan. In central Europe, breeds emerged such as the Bouvier (meaning 'drovers' dog') des Flandres, Bouvier des Ardennes, Bouvier de Roulers, Bouvier de Paret, Bouvier de Moerman (with only the Flanders and Ardennes dogs surviving), the Giant Schnauzer and the Hovawart. In Scandinavia, the long-extinct Dahlbo-hound, the size of an English Mastiff, was used to guard cattle in forest pastures. Lastly, where Europe and Asia meet, breeds now referred to as the Canaan Dog and the Anatolian Shepherd Dog, sometimes known as the Karabash, Akbash and Kangal dogs, developed.

Above: *Schnauzers, described in France as stable dogs from Germany. In England they would have been described as farmyard dogs.*

Left: *The Bouvier des Flandres, now used more by the police than by farmers.*

Below: *Anatolian Shepherd Dogs at work – huge powerful dogs with a strong flock-guarding instinct.*

White flock guardians are favoured in Italy, Greece, Hungary and Turkey.

Where did these flock-guarding breeds originate? The history of the dog is the history of mankind; when tribes migrated, their valuable flock-guarding dogs went with them. The flock-guarding breeds have three principal elements in common: their general appearance, their protective instincts and the fact that they are found wherever the Indo-Europeans settled. This area stretches from northern India through Iran into north-west Asia, eastern Europe, the northern Mediterranean countries, northern and western Europe to the British Isles, as well as in the southern hemisphere.

Three thousand years ago, the people from the area north of and between the Black and Caspian Seas, using their mastery of the horse and their invention of the wheeled chariot, migrated to the west, south-west, south-east and due south. Over the next thousand years or so, these mobile herdsmen were to spread out to form what eventually became the Celtic, Italic, German, Baltic, Illyrian, Thracian, Slav and Greek settlements. Extensive trade was conducted between Turkey, Portugal, Spain, southern Italy and Greece. Valuable hunting and flock-guarding dogs would have been coveted and then traded. Both agricultural and social changes affected the way the flock-guarding dogs developed and so, too, did climate and terrain. In Poland, for example, the Tatra Mountain Dog is a large thick-coated breed, whereas the Portuguese breed of Rafeiro do Alentejo is lighter coated but still sizeable. People's dependence on huge dogs to guard their livestock is not, however, as dramatic as their use in war and hunting and, because shepherds were not usually literate, these dogs rarely feature in the art or literature that have come down to us.

It is sad but perhaps inevitable that most of the flock-guarding dogs have been lost, including some distinct breed-types, through economic change and the extinction of many wild predators. Working dogs that wore spiked collars, had their ears cropped, fought wolves, gave birth to their pups in a hole in the ground and slept out of doors in the snow and chill wind deserved a better fate than becoming victim to misguided modern breed enthusiasts and their fads. In preserving those breeds that have survived we must remember the *essential* criteria that led to these flock-guarding dogs developing as such magnificent examples of the canine race: robustness, a functional physique, and size commensurate with soundness.

23

Up to 1000 BC about four-fifths of Europe north of the Alps and the Pyrenees was covered by dense forest. Over the next two hundred years extensive clearance by farmers provided the basis for economic growth through local trade, notably from the fairs dating from the reign of Charlemagne. This growth brought an unprecedented demand for herding dogs, both to control herds and get them to market. Bruges became the principal centre in Europe for the manufacture of woollen cloth, and medieval Flanders and its neighbours produced a wide range of driving dogs, as the Bouvier breeds demonstrate.

In the sixteenth century Spain had three million sheep and exported them both to her neighbours and to her new territories. The main trade was overland to France via the Pyrenees, with dogs playing a major role in their safe passage. Two hundred and fifty years ago, the Danes were sending eighty thousand head of cattle a year to Germany by driving them overland using dogs. The routes taken by the various drovers with their herding dogs crossed every European boundary, and it would be unwise to claim purity of descent for the different national breeds of today. These European drovers used dogs like the bouvier type and sharper, quicker dogs like the herding breeds of western Europe today.

These herding breeds have been just as neglected on the Continent as in Britain. In Belgium, for example, the four varieties of shepherd dog, named after the region of their development (Tervueren, Groenendael, Malinois and Laekenois) were unrecognised and not bred to type until the invaluable work of Professor Reul of the Cureghem Veterinary School bore fruit at the end of the nineteenth century. The Germans have lost their heeler: the red-brown cattle dog known as the Siegerlander Altdeutsche Hirtenhund or Kuhhund (cowdog). In modern Germany there is but one surviving breed of shepherd dog. Yet there were once distinct variations of it too: smooth-coated dogs; the white sheepdogs of Pomerania; the heavier-coated dogs of Bavaria and the south; and the lighter-coloured dogs of Prussia. In the early twentieth century wire-coated German Shepherd Dogs existed in the breed, with

The white sheepdogs of Pomerania, now out of favour but once imported by a British sheep farmer in the 1920s.

24

Above: *A Beauceron at work herding cattle in France.*

Right: *A Dutch short-haired sheepdog, typical of the pastoral dogs of the Low Countries.*

one well-known bitch of the 1920s, Lori Majer, featuring this coat texture, now no longer favoured. The Hutespitz, a big, thick-coated, white-and-fawn herding dog, was once widely used in northern Germany.

In Holland, however, they do favour a wire-haired shepherd dog, with a short-haired or smoother-haired and a long-haired variety too. In France, the Berger de Brie or Briard and the Picardy sheepdog represent their bouvier or drover's dog, and the Berger de Beauce or Beauceron equates to the German Shepherd Dog. The Briard is reputed to have accompanied Napoleon's armies, driving sheep for his quartermasters. Other French pastoral dogs, such as the Berger de Bresse, the Berger de Savoie, the Farou of Languedoc and the Labrit from Les Landes in the south-west, are probably now lost as breeds. Still surviving in northern Spain, however, is the Euskal Artzain Txakurra of the Bilbao region, now with its own preservation society, breed club and determinedly loyal fanciers.

In the more densely farmed areas of central France the shepherds had to keep close control of their flocks. They therefore used a team of dogs comprising one called the 'foot' dog to collect strays, another called the 'hand' dog to work close to the shepherd, and a third, known as the 'borders' dog, to patrol the perimeter of the grazing area. This last task demanded the most training, with the borders dog covering nearly 100 km (about 60 miles) each working day. French shepherds believed that double dew-claws on the hind legs denoted herding skill in a dog; the Beauceron features this unusual addition today.

In Hungary, the distinctive Puli, Pumi and Mudi breeds still perform as movers of livestock, with the much larger Komondor and Kuvasz breeds acting as flock guardians. The Scandinavians still have their herding dogs, of the classic spitz type of the Arctic north, and which are surprisingly similar in each country. The Icelandic Sheepdog is long established and very collie-like, as is the Buhund or 'cattle dog' of Norway, now becoming known in Britain's show rings. The Tooroochan Sheepdog

Above left: *The Mudi from Hungary, a small driving and herding breed.*
Above right: *The cattle-dog of Norway, typically 'spitz', i.e. prick-eared, foxy-headed and having a curly and bushy tail.*

of Siberia may now be lost as a distinct breed.

The Pyrenean Sheepdog comes in two varieties: smooth-faced and rough-faced. But as with so many herding breeds, this one could vary from one valley to the next. The Azun dog was more like a Schipperke of Belgium, the St-Beat dog was like a miniature Old English Sheepdog and the Ariège dog was much more muscular than either. Eventually the Arbazzie and Bagnères dogs were considered the type to be standardised.

The rough-faced Pyrenean Sheepdog is of the Beardie type, a breed-type also found in Catalonia as the Gos d'Atura, in Portugal as the Cao da Serra de Aires, in Egypt as the Armant, in Holland as the Schapendoes and in Poland as the Polski Owczarek Nizinny or Polish Lowland Sheepdog. The quaintly named 'sheep-poodle' of Germany, which displayed a corded coat, is probably now extinct. Known for centuries in Sardinia is the Fonni Sheepdog, a strongly made, goat-haired sheepdog, looking a little like a French Briard. The bearded sheepdog type is famous for its cleverness and quick response to training; the French army made good use of the Pyrenean dog as a messenger in the First World War.

Below left: *A Cao de Serra de Aires, the Portuguese 'Beardie', displaying classic bearded sheepdog features.*

Below right: *The Owczarek Nizinny, the sheepdog of the Polish lowlands. (The Tatra Mountain Dog operates in the highlands.)*

Left: *Sheepdogs in New Zealand pastures 6500 feet (2000 metres) above sea level, in the 1930s.*

This handsome Australian Shepherd Dog (right) may have been created from bob-tailed collies from the Black Mountains, on the borders of Wales and Herefordshire (below).

Right: *The Australian Kelpie, developed from dogs from Scotland in the nineteenth century.*

A different type of stock dog was required by settlers in the wide open spaces of America and Australia. Despite taking their herding dogs from Britain with them, the early colonists needed to adapt them to local conditions. In Australia this produced the Barb, the Kelpie and the Australian Cattle Dog. The striking resemblance to old forms of native British breeds in these emergent breeds is undeniable. The Australian Shepherd owes more to the United States for its development but is very similar to the bob-tailed sheepdogs of the Black Mountains. In New Zealand, the Huntaway was produced, a barker rather than a silent worker like the British collie, but still reminiscent of Britain's old black-and-tan sheepdog.

The Swedish Vastgotsaspets or Vallhund ('dog of the home pasture'), a heeling breed very like the Corgis and heelers of Great Britain.

In the United States, a survey in the 1940s revealed that their most numerous breed was the humble farm collie, still looking much like its British ancestor. One American Kennel Club recognises these dogs as a formal breed, known as the English Shepherd. There is also a breed called the McNab Dog, a smooth collie descended from sheepdogs taken to California in 1885. But inevitably the Americans needed to meet their own requirements, and a breed such as the Catahoula Leopard Dog was created. Catahoulas are essentially gathering dogs, having a natural tendency to circle to the other side of stock, opposite the handler. They specialise in gathering rough wild cattle and even hogs. They track the stock, bring it to bay rather as a hound would, bark loudly to attract the stockmen and often work in teams. They are reminiscent of the Portuguese Cattle Dog, Cao de Castro Laboreiro, which has a comparable function as a herd-protector and drover.

The Americans have produced their own shepherd dog, the Shiloh Shepherd, which they claim is more like the old-style German Shepherd Dog, heavier boned, more heavily coated and more muscular than the modern German dog. It could be that in such a way old farm breeds are restored to their original type. The American and Australian pastoral breeds are certainly more robust than some of the British. It would be a worthy action if some enthusiast were to attempt the re-creation of the Old Welsh Grey sheepdog using the blood of the Patagonian Sheepdog or Barboucho. This dog is believed to have descended from the old Welsh breed after Welsh settlers took their dogs with them to the Chubut valley in the nineteenth century.

The Atlas Sheepdog of Morocco, also known as the Aidi or Kabyle Dog, is a rarity – a pastoral breed of non-European origin. The Kabyles were the aboriginal people of Barbary and kept sheep, cattle, goats, camels and donkeys. Employed as drovers but with a nasty reputation as guard dogs, their dogs are prized for their versatility and are selectively bred for their alertness and aggression. Another ancient breed, the Canaan Dog of Israel, was restored literally from the wild by Dr Menzel in the late 1930s. She found amongst the feral dogs of what was then Palestine a distinct collie strain, believed to be abandoned herding dogs of the Bedouin. Once restored by a careful breeding programme, they excelled as guide dogs for the blind, sentry and messenger dogs and in sheepdog trials; four hundred of them were trained for mine detection work in the Second World War.

Strangely, the Canaan Dog has a definite spitz look to it, featuring the bushy curled tail and prick ears of the northern dogs. The northern Scandinavian herding dogs range from the corgi-like to the collie-like, with the Norwegian Senjahund and

A Dutch brindle holding dog, typical of the European breeds that 'hold', 'grip' or 'pin', which were later misused as baiting dogs in the bull ring.

the Swedish Vastgotaspets or Vallhund exemplifying the former, and the Maastehund of the Lofoten Islands, the Finnish Herder and the Lapponian Herder resembling the latter. The corgi-type heelers have to be agile, quick and alert, if only to survive. As cattle dogs, they have to learn to bite the hind foot that is bearing weight, giving them that extra split second to duck or flatten to avoid the reacting hefty kick. They learn, too, to attack alternate feet, rather than repeating their first attempt, in order to cause a little more surprise.

The Sicilians developed a cattle dog, called the Branchiero, which worked in a unique way, leaping at the head of the herd leader to turn it in the required direction. It resembled the Rottweiler, another former cattle dog and also alternatively called 'Butcher's Dog'. Stockmen and butchers have long had a need for powerful dogs that could hold, pin or grip wayward cattle, difficult rams or highly determined boars, especially in places where the herd ran semi-wild. Predictably, they opted to employ 'catch' or 'capture' dogs from the hunting field. These dogs developed from the hunting mastiffs used by primitive hunters to pull down aurochs, buffalo and boar before the invention of firearms.

These holding dogs were used quite extensively as the surviving breeds illustrate: the Bullmastiff in Britain, the Dogue de Bordeaux in France, the Alano in Spain, the Fila (literally 'seizing' or 'pinning' dog) Brasileiro of Brazil, the Neapolitan Mastiff (sometimes called the Cane de Presa or 'dog that grips') and Cane Corso of Italy, the Perro de Presa (literally 'gripping' dog) Canario and the Perro de Presa Mallorquin, from the Canaries and Majorca respectively. In modern America, a breed called the American Bulldog, although more like a Bullmastiff than a Bulldog, is still used to catch hogs, a very dangerous activity and one in which the dog can be killed. These huge, very resolute dogs hurl themselves at the hog, which weighs three times their weight, and seize it by the ear, hanging on despite every effort of the enraged hog to shake them off or harm them. The sheer, almost reckless, bravery of such dogs is quite remarkable.

Farmers throughout the world needed small dogs too: to control pests such as rats, to act as turnspit dogs in the farmhouse kitchen and to go to ground when foxes were hunted. The smallest could do all three tasks but had to be very small to fit into the cage round the spit and work the treadmill without too much discomfort. In Britain, the work was considered too arduous to be done on successive days and so a team of dogs was used, leading to the expression 'every dog has his day'. In Germany, small pinschers were used, similar to the modern breed of Miniature

29

A French farmer with his all-purpose 'cur-dog', able to herd sheep, catch rats and warn of the presence of strangers.

Pinscher. The German breed of Schnauzer is a classic example of a versatile farm breed: the Riesenschnauzer or Giant Schnauzer was the drover and farm guard, the standard Schnauzer was the yard dog, and the miniature version the ratter.

In Russia, the Laika breeds offered a similar versatility, the large ones acting as herders and the small ones as yard dogs and ratters. In America, they developed their own 'Rat Terrier', a small, mainly white terrier weighing from 7 pounds (3.2 kg) to twice that. This breed is now recognised as a distinct breed, as is the slightly bigger Brazilian Terrier, a renowned farm ratting dog.

All over the world, dogs, whether employed to drive cattle, sheep, goats or reindeer, to guard farmsteads or flocks, to kill foxes or rats, or to hold an individual animal, were bred with just one object in mind: their function. This criterion, ruthlessly pursued, demanded of the dogs physical and mental soundness, robustness of health and responsiveness to training. We no longer pursue that objective in the developed world, and everyday our crowded veterinary surgeries demonstrate our foolishness.

The future

The decline in British farming, hill farming especially, casts a shadow over the future of working farm dogs. However, the work of a number of different bodies gives cause for optimism. The International Sheepdog Society continues to foster sheepdog trials and promote working dogs. The Border Collie clubs are promoting a working certificate for their show dogs. In Germany, the German Shepherd Dog is being worked again, with herding trials each September. In Australia, the Yarrowview Veterinary Hospital in Victoria has a programme to 'improve the quality and working performance of the rural farm working sheep, cattle and goat dogs'. In the United States, the use of flock-guarding breeds increases annually. More and more show fanciers are becoming interested in working dogs from the pastoral breeds. Information on such activities can be found in the weekly canine press, for example *Our Dogs* and *Dog World*, the farming press and countryside and sporting magazines like *The Field*. The television series *One Man and His Dog* attracted sizeable and loyal audiences.

The dogs which compete at sheepdog trials, however, are not bred to be pets; they are hyperactive, with an irrepressible desire to work, which can conflict with contemporary urban lifestyles. This desire to work, in all the various farm dog breeds, whether huge and shaggy or small and sleek, is what makes them so useful to man in other spheres. The Belgian Malinois used by the German police, the German Shepherd Dog in the British police, the Beauceron with the French police and the Canaan Dog with the Israeli Armed Forces all illustrate this usefulness today. Farm dogs are the unglamorous, unsung heroes of the canine world. We have every reason to be thankful for their support and loyalty to us and to do what we can to ensure a good future for them.

The collie typifies the farmer's dog: unexaggerated, uncomplicated, forever alert and renowned for its faithfulness.

Further reading

Bewick, Thomas. *A General History of Quadrupeds*. Walker, 1807.

Clutton-Brock, Juliet. *Domestic Animals from Early Times*. British Museum and Heinemann, 1981.

Combe, Iris. *Herding Dogs – Their Origins and Development in Britain*. Faber & Faber, 1987.

Dalziel, Hugh. *British Dogs: Volume II*. Upcott Gill, 1897.

Hancock, David. *The Heritage of the Dog*. Nimrod, 1990.

Hancock, David. *Old Working Dogs*. Shire, 1984; reprinted 1998.

Holmes, John. *The Farmer's Dog*. Popular Dogs, 1975.

Hubbard, Clifford. *Working Dogs of the World*. Sidgwick & Jackson, 1947.

Moorhouse, Sydney. *The British Sheepdog*. Witherby, 1950.

Shaw, Vero. *The Illustrated Book of the Dog*. Cassell, 1881.

Toulson, Shirley. *The Drovers*. Shire, 1980; reprinted 1988.

Walsh, J. H. *The Dogs of the British Islands*. The Field, 1878.

William Pease (born 1880) with his farm collie 'Fly' at West Tilbury. Farm collies of this type, even with the same name, can be found on farms today.